I0815094

SAN DIEGO CHARGERS

BY TODD KORTEMEIER

SportsZone
An Imprint of Abdo Publishing
abdopublishing.com

abdopublishing.com

Published by Abdo Publishing, a division of ABDO, PO Box 398166, Minneapolis, Minnesota 55439.

Printed in the United States of America, North Mankato, Minnesota
042016
092016

Cover Photo: Matt Rourke/AP Images
Interior Photos: Matt Rourke/AP Images, 1; G. Paul Burnett/AP Images, 4-5; Bill Kostroun/AP Images, 6-7; Bettmann/Corbis, 8-9, 12; Pro Football Hall of Fame/AP Images, 10, 11, 13; Pro Football Hall of Fame/AP Images, 11; AP Images, 14-15; Clem Murray/AP Images, 16-17; Paul Spinelli/AP Images, 18-19; Kevin Terrell/AP Images, 20; Damian Strohmeyer/AP Images, 21; Paul Sancya/AP Images, 22-23; Jeff Roberson/AP Images, 24; G. Newman Lowrance/AP Images, 25; Scott Boehm/AP Images, 26-27; John Bazemore/AP Images, 28-29

Editor: Patrick Donnelly
Series Designer: Nikki Farinella

Cataloging-in-Publication Data
Names: Kortemeier, Todd, author.
Title: San Diego Chargers / by Todd Kortemeier.
Description: Minneapolis, MN : Abdo Publishing, [2017] | Series: NFL up close | Includes index.
Identifiers: LCCN 2015960452 | ISBN 9781680782318 (lib. bdg.) | ISBN 9781680776423 (ebook)
Subjects: LCSH: San Diego Chargers (Football team)--History--Juvenile literature. | National Football League--Juvenile literature. | Football--Juvenile literature. | Professional sports--Juvenile literature. | Football teams--California--Juvenile literature.
Classification: DDC 796.332--dc23
LC record available at http://lccn.loc.gov/2015960452

TABLE OF CONTENTS

SUPER CHARGERS

Time was running out on the 1994 San Diego Chargers. They had made a surprise run to the American Football Conference (AFC) Championship Game. But on the road against the heavily favored Pittsburgh Steelers, the Chargers suffered a power outage.

The Steelers dominated the game well into the third quarter. The Chargers' offense could not get anything going. But their defense kept the score close. Pittsburgh led only 13-3. Late in the third quarter, San Diego quarterback Stan Humphries found tight end Alfred Pupunu wide open for a 43-yard touchdown. The Chargers were back in business.

Chargers quarterback Stan Humphries throws a pass against the Steelers in the AFC Championship Game.

12
NIKE

Now it was the Steelers' turn to struggle on offense. San Diego finally took advantage. With just over five minutes left, Humphries connected with wide receiver Tony Martin on another 43-yard touchdown pass to give the Chargers a 17–13 lead.

The Steelers had one last chance. Quarterback Neil O'Donnell drove them down to the Chargers' 3-yard line. On fourth down, O'Donnell threw a pass into the end zone. Chargers linebacker Dennis Gibson dived in front of the receiver and knocked the ball away. The Chargers were headed to their first Super Bowl.

Chargers defenders Leslie O'Neal, *91*, and Chris Mims put the pressure on Steelers quarterback Neil O'Donnell.

Tony Martin, *right*, and Mark Seay celebrate Martin's go-ahead touchdown in the fourth quarter against the Steelers.

FAST FACT

The Chargers faced another heavily favored team in the Super Bowl. They lost the Super Bowl. They lost to the San Francisco 49ers 49–26.

FAST FACT

The Chargers constantly battled poor attendance in Los Angeles. Their division-clinching win over the Denver Broncos drew fewer than 10,000 fans.

Like most other Chargers home games in Los Angeles, this November 1960 game against the Houston Oilers was played in front of thousands of empty seats.

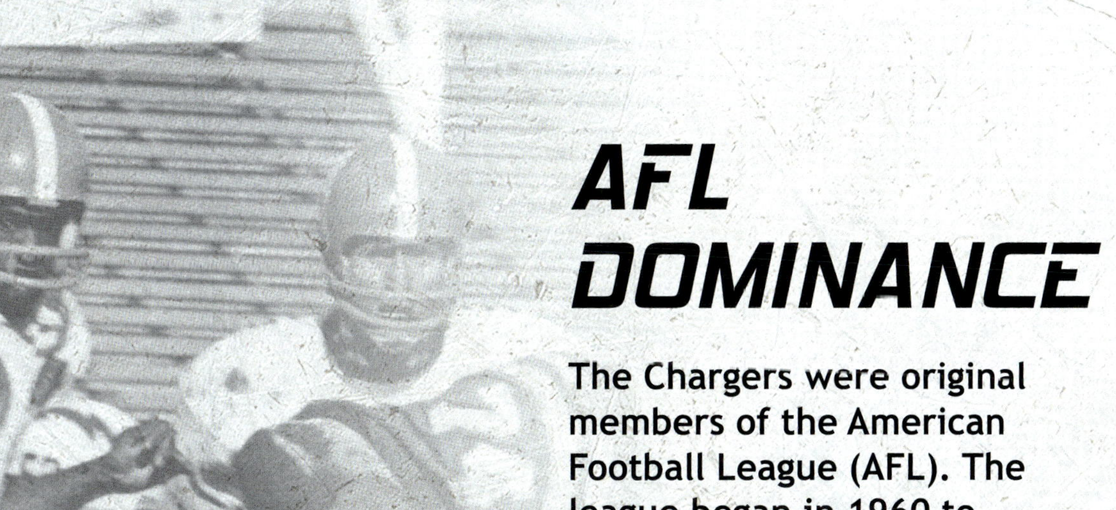

AFL DOMINANCE

The Chargers were original members of the American Football League (AFL). The league began in 1960 to challenge the National Football League (NFL). The Chargers' first owner, Barron Hilton, placed his team in Los Angeles. Their electrifying nickname was displayed through lightning bolts on uniforms in their team colors—gold, blue, and white.

With Jack Kemp at quarterback, the first Chargers team had a high-flying offense. They scored a combined 184 points in their final four regular-season games and surged to the AFL title game.

Despite their success, the Chargers were not as popular in Los Angeles as the NFL's Rams. So after losing the AFL title game to the Houston Oilers, Hilton decided to move his team south to San Diego.

The move did not slow the Chargers down one bit. They were known for their outstanding passing attack. In 1963, San Diego went 11-3 in the regular season and won the AFL West Division title. The Chargers faced the Boston Patriots in the AFL Championship Game. In two regular-season wins over the Patriots, San Diego had managed just 24 total points. But in the title game, the Chargers rolled up 610 yards in total offense and scored seven touchdowns. Their 51-10 rout of the Patriots gave them their first—and only—AFL championship.

Chargers coach Sid Gillman takes in the action with quarterback John Hadl in 1962.

Wide receiver Lance Alworth was one of San Diego's early stars. Graceful and speedy, the future Hall of Famer topped 1,000 receiving yards for seven straight years (1963–1969). Alworth helped quarterback John Hadl lead the league in passing yards three times. The last came in 1971, after the Chargers and the rest of the AFL had joined the NFL.

John Hadl, *left*, and Sid Gillman discuss strategy in 1971.

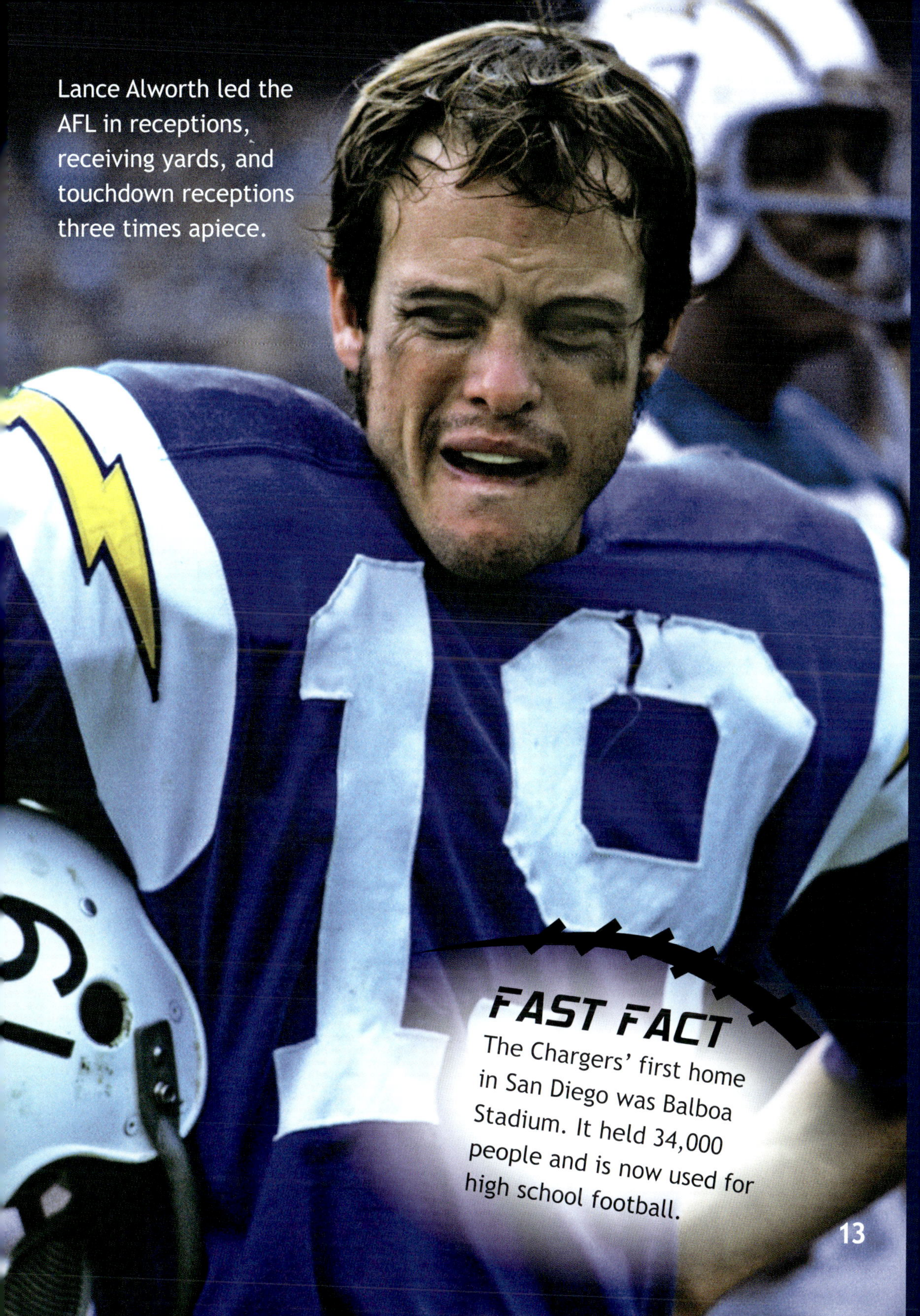

Lance Alworth led the AFL in receptions, receiving yards, and touchdown receptions three times apiece.

FAST FACT

The Chargers' first home in San Diego was Balboa Stadium. It held 34,000 people and is now used for high school football.

Dan Fouts is the only player to lead the NFL in passing yards four straight seasons.

AIR CORYELL

In a time when most teams still focused on running the ball, coach Sid Gillman's Chargers passed it all over the field. The AFL was credited with popularizing a faster-paced, more exciting brand of football. Gillman's Chargers were a big part of that trend.

The Chargers struggled in the early 1970s, after the AFL had merged with the NFL. Then, coach Don Coryell arrived and reminded Chargers fans of the team's high-flying AFL days. His offense was called "Air Coryell" because he let his quarterbacks throw a lot of passes. Strong-armed Dan Fouts was a perfect fit to run it. In 1979, Coryell's first full season as San Diego's coach, Fouts set an NFL record by passing for at least 300 yards in four straight games.

FAST FACT

The Air Coryell teams could score by running the ball, too. Chuck Muncie had 39 rushing touchdowns from 1981 to 1983.

The Chargers had plenty of great receivers, too. Tight end Kellen Winslow and wide receiver Charlie Joiner reached the Pro Football Hall of Fame, as did Fouts. The 1981 Chargers might have been their best team. Fouts threw for 4,802 yards, and they scored 478 points. They survived an overtime thriller against the Miami Dolphins to open the playoffs. Then, they went to Cincinnati to play the Bengals for a chance to go to the Super Bowl.

The game later became known as "the Freezer Bowl." It was one of the coldest games in NFL history, with wind chills bottoming out at minus-59 degrees Fahrenheit (-51°C). The weather kept Air Coryell grounded, and the Chargers lost to the Bengals 27-7.

Dan Fouts's face is hidden behind a cloud of steam during the Chargers' "Freezer Bowl" loss at Cincinnati.

Chargers tight end Kellen Winslow led the NFL in receptions in 1980 and 1981.

FAST FACT

The Chargers moved into San Diego Stadium in 1967. It later became known as Jack Murphy Stadium and then Qualcomm Stadium.

SAY OW!

Don Coryell left the Chargers in 1986. Dan Fouts retired after the 1987 season. He held most of the Chargers' team passing records at the time. But despite putting up consistently great numbers, Fouts could not get the Chargers to the Super Bowl. Without the two men who put Air Coryell on the map, the Chargers' offense slipped toward the bottom of the league rankings.

Their offensive decline was met with an increased focus on defense in San Diego. The Chargers used their first-round draft pick in 1990 on linebacker Junior Seau. He was tough, intimidating, and popular with his teammates. The Chargers' defense turned around under Seau's leadership.

The Chargers shifted their focus from offense to defense with the arrival of linebacker Junior Seau in 1990.

The Chargers made three playoff appearances in the 1990s. In 1994, they went to the Super Bowl for the first time, losing to the San Francisco 49ers. That Chargers team thrived without passing the ball much. They got 1,350 rushing yards from Natrone Means, a punishing young running back. They also relied on Seau and the rest of the hard-working defense.

Natrone Means was a bruising running back who led the Chargers in rushing three times.

FAST FACT

The 1992 Chargers lost their first four games but finished 11-5. They were the first team to start 0-4 and come back to make the playoffs.

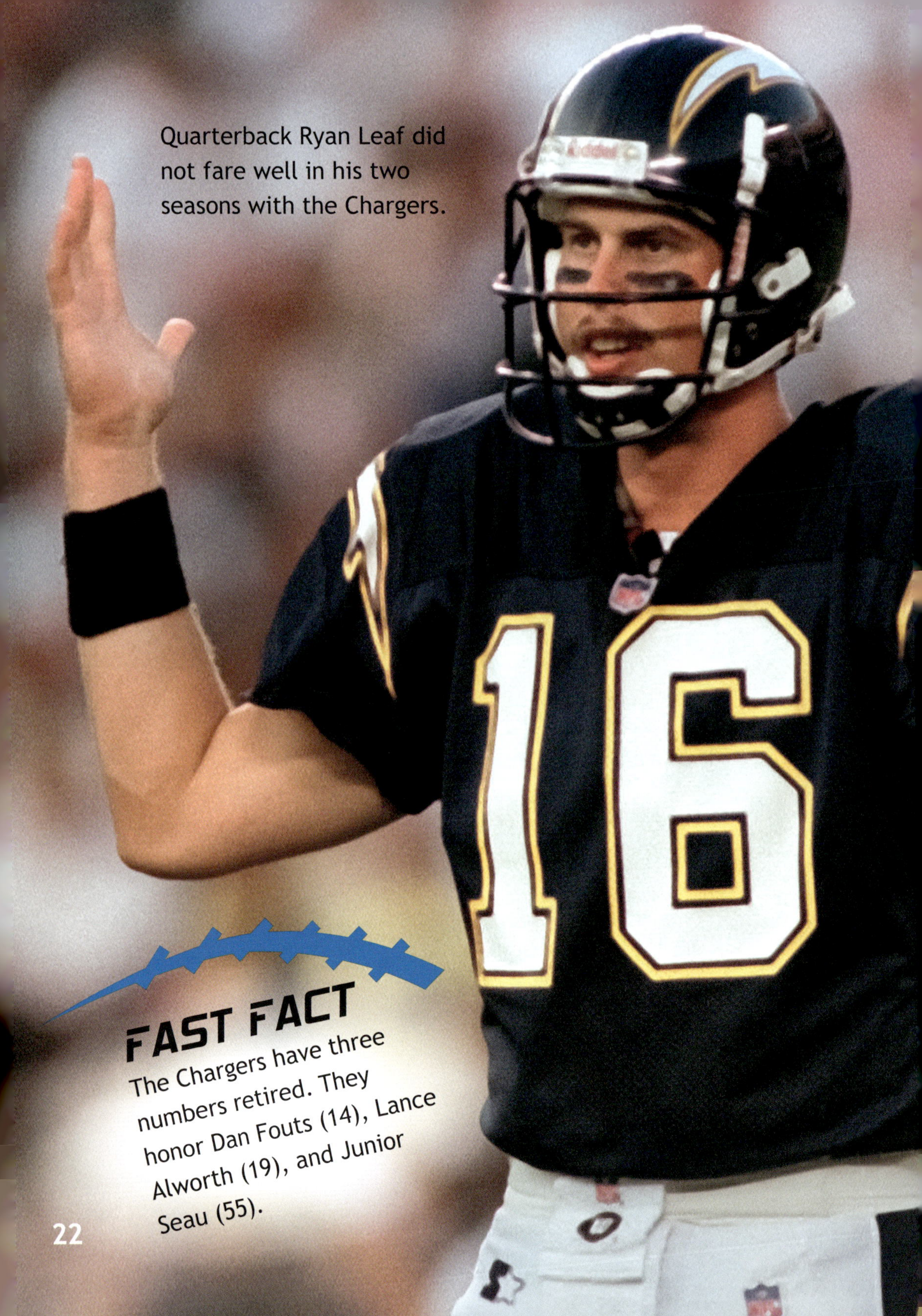

Quarterback Ryan Leaf did not fare well in his two seasons with the Chargers.

FAST FACT

The Chargers have three numbers retired. They honor Dan Fouts (14), Lance Alworth (19), and Junior Seau (55).

After the Super Bowl season, the Chargers hit another rocky stretch. They went 4-12 in 1997, the second-worst record in the NFL that year. They turned their focus to improving through the 1998 NFL Draft. The Indianapolis Colts held the first pick. The Chargers had the second pick. That year, two quarterback prospects had risen to the top of the charts. The Colts took Peyton Manning from Tennessee. That left Ryan Leaf from Washington State for the Chargers.

Leaf was a disaster. In parts of two seasons with the Chargers, he threw 13 touchdown passes and 33 interceptions. His failure left the Chargers in search of a quarterback again. This time, however, they had much more success in the draft.

LaDainian Tomlinson starred for nine years in San Diego.

FRIGHTENING LIGHTNING

The low point in Chargers history came in 2000. The team won just one game. But their first two picks in the 2001 NFL Draft became all-time greats. They took running back LaDainian Tomlinson with the fifth pick overall. Then, with the first pick in the second round, they landed quarterback Drew Brees.

Tomlinson was a versatile star from the start. He ran for 1,236 yards as a rookie. It was the first of eight straight 1,000-yard seasons. He proved to be an excellent receiver, too. In his third season, Tomlinson caught 100 passes. That is rare for a running back. He even threw seven touchdown passes in his career. Brees started off slowly. But by his third year, he and the Chargers were the best team in their division.

The 2004 Chargers went 12-4, their best record since 1979. On a snowy, late-December day in Cleveland, the Chargers shut out the Browns 21-0 to clinch the division. It was their first division title in 10 years. But in the playoffs, they lost a heartbreaker in overtime to the New York Jets.

Brees left through free agency after the 2005 season. The Chargers had drafted quarterback Philip Rivers in 2004. After backing up Brees for two seasons, Rivers took over the starting job in 2006 and led the Chargers to a 14-2 record, the best in team history. But they suffered yet another crushing playoff defeat as the New England Patriots rallied from eight points down in the fourth quarter for a 24-21 victory.

Super Bowl-winning quarterback Drew Brees began his career with the Chargers.

FAST FACT

LaDainian Tomlinson played with the Chargers through the 2009 season. He is their all-time leader with 12,490 rushing yards.

Rivers became one of the best quarterbacks in football. He led the Chargers to the playoffs every year from 2006 through 2009. They even made the conference championship after the 2007 season but lost again to the Patriots. Like Dan Fouts before him, Rivers flourished in a potent passing attack. Chargers fans are hopeful that someday soon the team will bring a championship to San Diego.

Philip Rivers airs one out against the Kansas City Chiefs in 2015.

FAST FACT

The Chargers signed rookie tight end Antonio Gates in 2003. He made the Pro Bowl every year from 2004 to 2011.

Antonio Gates hauls in a touchdown pass against the Jacksonville Jaguars in 2015.

TIMELINE

1960
The Los Angeles Chargers play their first season in the AFL.

1961
The Chargers move south down Interstate 5 to San Diego.

1964
On January 5, the Chargers beat the Boston Patriots 51-10 in San Diego for their first AFL championship.

1981
Under the "Air Coryell" offense, quarterback Dan Fouts sets a single-season NFL record with 4,802 passing yards.

1982
On January 10 in frigid Cincinnati, the Chargers come up one game short of the Super Bowl, losing to the Bengals in "the Freezer Bowl."

1995
After upsetting the Pittsburgh Steelers to reach their first Super Bowl, the Chargers lose to the San Francisco 49ers 49-26 on January 29.

2001
The Chargers draft running back LaDainian Tomlinson. He rushes for at least 1,000 yards in each of his first eight NFL seasons.

2006
First-year starter Philip Rivers leads the Chargers to a team-best 14-2 record, and Tomlinson wins NFL Most Valuable Player Award.

GLOSSARY

CONFERENCE
A group of divisions that help form a league.

DIVISION
A group of teams that help form a league.

DRAFT
The process by which teams select players who are new to the league.

FREE AGENT
A player who is free to sign with any team.

OVERTIME
An extra period or periods played in the event of a tie.

PLAYOFFS
A set of games played after the regular season that decides which team will be the champion.

PROSPECT
An athlete likely to succeed at the next level.

RETIRE
To withdraw from a job or occupation.

ROOKIE
A first-year player.

INDEX

ABOUT THE AUTHOR

Todd Kortemeier has authored dozens of books for young people, primarily on sports topics. He is a graduate of the University of Minnesota's School of Journalism & Mass Communication and lives near Minneapolis with his wife.